SMASH
THE **BOTTLENECK**

SMASH
THE BOTTLENECK

HOW TO IMPROVE CRITICAL PROCESS EFFICIENCIES FOR DRAMATICALLY INCREASED KEY RESULTS

RAY HODGE
THE EFFICIENT TRADE BUSINESS SERIES

Edited by Melanie Nicholson

Fig 1.10: Process Example - *Courtesy of simPRO Software Group*

Front Page Photo - Courtesy of Johnny Chung Lee © 2006

Layout and Design by Julie Csizmadia
CsizMEDIA - Creative Design Solutions

ISBN: 978-0-9943138-0-5

TABLE OF CONTENTS

3 Policies, Processes and Procedures and Systems

THE DIFFERENCE BETWEEN CHAOS AND ORDER

Distinctions 57

Policy Document .59

Process Example .60

Procedure Example 61

System Example .62

Writing Excellent Business Systems 63

From the Shelf to the Shop Floor 64

IN CONCLUSION 67

APPENDIX .69

Case Study 69

Introduction 69

Stage One: Analysis – Current Process and Results . 70

Stage Two: Process Redesign 71

Stage Three: Implementation 72

Stage Four: Monitoring and Recording Progress . . . 72

Stage Five: Manage New Processes 73

Results 73

WHAT OTHERS ARE SAYING ABOUT THIS BOOK

"After working with over 400 contractors in the past decade I would firmly recommend this booklet as a must read for any trade business that has passed its honeymoon period and is looking for answers. Ray's experience with the industry is evident and the steps to take your business to the next level are laid out in manageable stages. This booklet provides insight and a sense of sanity to any industry which is often fraught with stress and frustration. What a great way to start taking charge, get your business back on track, and go back to loving the reason why you went into business in the first place."

- ROB FRANCIS - BUSINESS DEVELOPMENT MANAGER QLD: simPRO SOFTWARE GROUP

"Helping business "smash the bottleneck" is exactly what Ray does. When your business is more efficient you get into the flow and save on costs, improve customer satisfaction and increase profits. His message is easy to read, digest, and apply with a focus on designing efficient process around customers needs and expectations. Key concepts are easy to understand with Ray's real world examples."

- ADRIAN HART - CHIEF EXECUTIVE OFFICER: SWIMMING POOL & SPA ASSOCIATION OF QUEENSLAND INC.

"Well formulated, hits the mark for the intended audience with useful case studies, and real life examples."

- AMANDA DAWES - BUSINESS DEVELOPMENT MANAGER MASTER PAINTERS AND DECORATORS AUSTRALIA

About the Author

Ray Hodge speaks and consults to businesses and organizations, a notable event being the Department of the Australian Prime Minister and Cabinet. Ray has held positions as General Manager in the Tourism and Construction industries and has successfully run his own businesses in the Finance, Property and Accommodation sectors. His main work in the last 25 years has been in senior management, leadership development, coaching and finance. His current speaking and consulting focus is a convergence of these areas combined with his natural abilities in identifying key hotspots within an organization and the improvement of such.

Much of Ray's current work is focused on improving the critical efficiencies within companies and organizations to dramatically increase key results. These critical efficiencies may lie in any area of an organization including finance, processes, people, sales, marketing, etc. He has found that if you identify the one or two key areas that are significantly having a negative impact on results and then rectify those areas, the results are often substantial and affect broader areas. As he likes to say "the one impacting the many."

Introduction

In my extensive work with service-based businesses, one of the common issues they all experience at sometime in their life is that of the bottleneck. Things begin to jam up and this is often, oddly enough, success related. Whether you provide trade services, insurance, legal, accounting or other forms of business services, you offer invaluable work with very defined processes of delivery. Along with these processes, you also have people at the various process points ensuring that accurate and timely delivery takes place.

The common story for many businesses is that the owner was working for someone else, saw how much the boss was charging compared to how much he was being paid and thought, "I might as well go and start my own show." They start their business with the dual goal of more money and more free time. FREEDOM!

They put an advertisement in the yellow pages, the local paper, and get some brochures delivered and spread the word among their friends. Work starts flowing in. Over time they gain a steady stream of business and make more money than they were previously earning. So far so good.

Due to the fact that their work is generally of a high standard, referrals and repeat business start to flow in. This takes them to the point of needing to hire others, which then creates the necessity of extra paperwork and administration. They employ extra workers, often with their 'significant other' coming in to relieve the administrative load, and now they have progressed from one person to a few in a short period of time.

The challenges of an increasing workload, managing their people, ever increasing administrative requirements, and ensuring there is enough money in the bank to pay everyone at week's end, gradually creates a negative impact. Before long the initial goals of more money and more time become a distant dream. Things start to back up.

Customers start to complain about the service, lagging time frames, quality of work and errors in billings. Cash flow starts to become challenged as customers take advantage of the fact that they aren't being chased. Employees start to feel the strain with the owners' partner considers stepping aside as "this isn't what I signed up for." What used to be a relatively easy business has now become a machine that needs constant maintenance and refueling to continue.

The following tends to eventuate:

- Excellent workmanship is sacrificed to speed of completion
- Pro-active business now becomes a re-active business
- Chasing more work becomes a constant necessity
- The fire and passion for their new business begins to wane
- Chaos replaces order
- The dream becomes a nightmare

The fundamental issue I have observed is that over time, businesses get to varying states of chaos that create increased load on current systems and processes. The chaos, as I mentioned, is often the result of doing things well and achieving success. So that's the positive. The negative is that chaos eventually forges a path of discontentment from the customer through to employees and, eventually, to you the business owner.

This book addresses the bottleneck effect, in the following areas:

- Understanding the root causes of blocked process and flow
- The importance of the customer in relation to our internal processes
- How to smash the bottleneck to get things flowing
- A simple way of systemizing business systems

As a final note, the principles outlined here come from application not theory so take them, use them, adapt them to your own situation. I've seen them work countless times and if applied with diligence and discipline, will get you back to enjoying your business.

Good luck!

1

Map Your Process

ALIGNING BUSINESS PROCESS WITH CUSTOMER EXPECTATIONS

Businesses reach varying degrees of chaos at different stages in their life. More often than not, this is the result of success. The combination of exceptional work, broadening of offerings, success in marketing initiatives and referrals from satisfied customers all flow with ease for periods of time. Customers are happy, employees content, cash flow is good and everything rolls along with little resistance. As this builds at the top end, incoming calls related to existing and new work increase, along with new opportunities to explore. This then creates the necessary administrative duties that come with that success.

With the increase of inputs comes a corresponding load on the business systems and processes. The outputs just can't keep up. The incoming flow invariably builds up, creating a bottleneck effect. Figure 1.0 on the following page demonstrates this.

Success Inputs
Quality work and
marketing initiatives
increase demand

SUCCESS

Factors
- Increased load on
processes and people
- No accountability
- People not suited
to roles
- Owner/managers
fear letting go

Effects
- Complaints
- Timeframes
increase
- Dissatisfaction
- Invoicing delays
- Low cash flow
- Employees
leave

CHAOS

Increased work capacity, employee and customer satisfaction, flow in processes, sales and profit, discretionary time for the owner.

FLOW

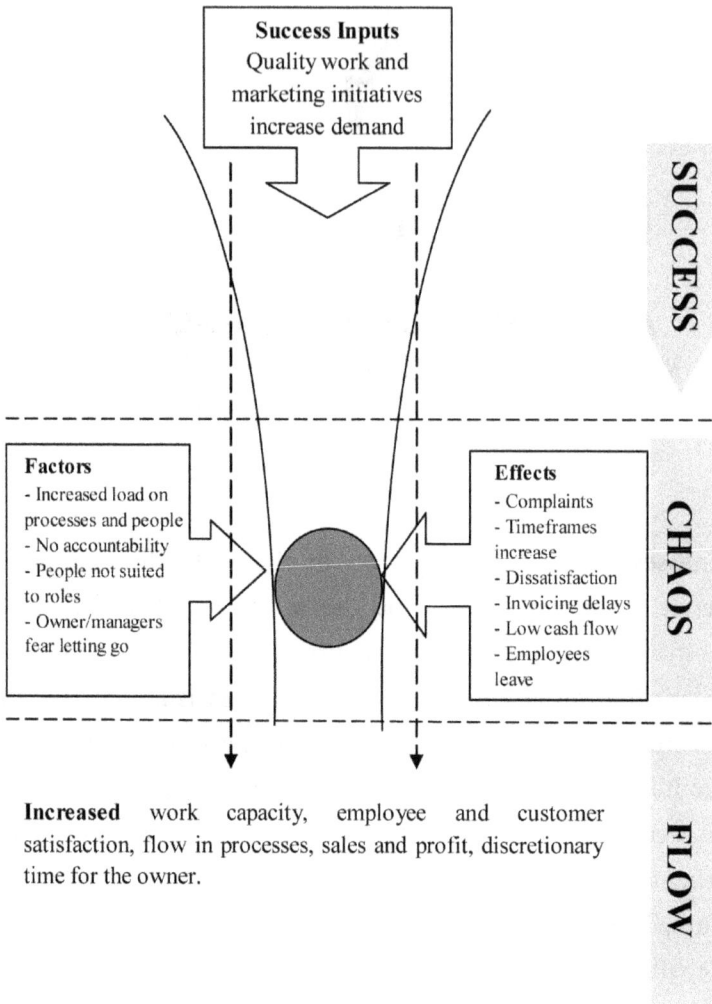

Fig 1.0: The Bottleneck Effect

Once the incoming flow builds to a certain volume, the effects generally tend to be:

- Lengthier turnaround times

- Slow response to incoming calls

- Cash flow becomes a cash trickle

- Growing piles of paperwork

- Disgruntled employees

- Increase in client complaints

You get the picture. The systems aren't keeping up, resulting in the second stage being chaos. Here's another way of looking at it.

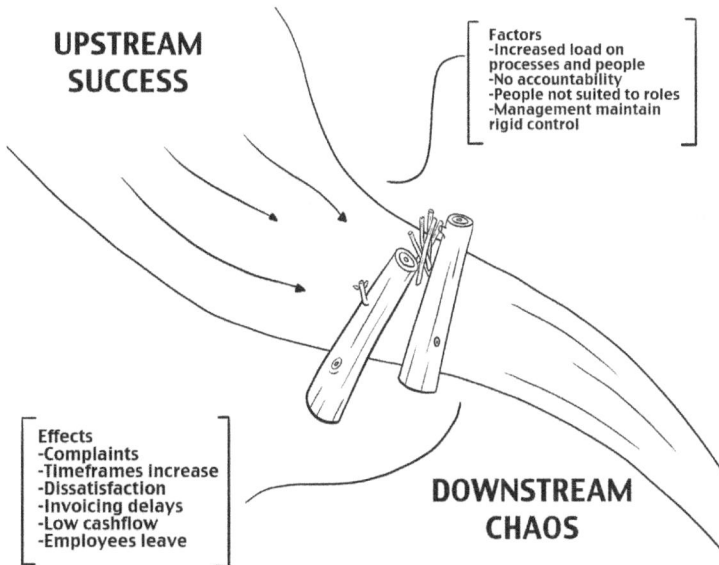

UPSTREAM SUCCESS

Factors
-Increased load on processes and people
-No accountability
-People not suited to roles
-Management maintain rigid control

Effects
-Complaints
-Timeframes increase
-Dissatisfaction
-Invoicing delays
-Low cashflow
-Employees leave

DOWNSTREAM CHAOS

Fig 1.1: The Log Jam Effect

The aim of this book is to identify the root causes that may be creating the bottleneck effect and then to create the key systems and processes to restore flow to the organization.

FIRST THINGS FIRST: MEASURE CURRENT RESULTS

At the start of any change process, it's important to take some baseline measurements to define our starting place. When we focus on losing weight, our personal trainer will take initial measurements (scary as that is). Along the way, they continue to check our current progress against the initial starting place. According to the data from their ongoing measurements they can make adjustments along the way. Company and organizational change management is no different.

What Do I Measure?

Every industry has its own key indicators and following are some standard areas that are worth measuring for trade service companies. Some are process related, others more general and this list is not exhaustive.

Financial – General	Defects / Errors / Reworks
Revenue	Client complaints
Cost of goods sold	Error #
Gross Profit	Rework hours
Expenses	Error cost
Net Profit	**Marketing and Sales**
End of month bank balance	Number of enquiries
Productivity and Billings	Source of enquiries e.g. Google
Tradesman: Total Monthly $	Referral #
Average hourly rate $	**Debtors / WIP / Write offs-ons**
Total company – ave hour rate $	Current debtors
Hours billed against hours worked	Debtors - 56+ - $
Hours billed against hours paid	Debtor days
Avg. dollar sale	WIP

As you can see, there are a myriad of things you can measure. At first it can be a little overwhelming but doing the hard yards of capturing some of this information allows you to get control of things. Many businesses have no idea how they are progressing. As long as there is money in the bank to pay next week's wages things are good. For true progress to take place you need a baseline to measure against. Without this you won't know if you are truly improving.

When compiling results, I find it helpful to collate information from the previous twelve months and then take the average in all areas. If you are experiencing rapid growth, use the last six months or last quarter. This then forms the starting place for improvement. All change that is implemented from this point on can be measured against the average of the previous selected period.

One of the tools I have found most helpful for this is a Key Performance Indicator chart that I have developed for gathering key information. I have only used financial data as an example here but it can include anything else you want to measure. Figure 1.2 demonstrates this.

KEY PERFORMANCE INDICATORS					
	Current Avg	Improvement Goal	Jun	Jul	Aug
Financial					
Revenue					
COGS					
GP					
Expenses					
Net Profit					
Debtors / WIP / Write offs-ons					
Current debtors - goal twice monthly revenue					
Debtors - 56+ - $					
Debtors - 56+ %					
Debtor days					
Debtors against WIP %					

Figure 1.2: Key Performance Indicator Chart

From the KPI chart, you now have the data collated from the previous period in the average column along (which is a monthly figure) with a column to establish an improvement goal for each area. It is important to note that the collation of this data, both from a historical perspective and then the ongoing input of throughout the year, gives you a great perspective on your business and the best thing about it is, you have the key data of your entire business all on one sheet.

Many business owners will be presented with their profit and loss/balance sheets at the end of the month. They might review them quickly, see if they made a profit or a loss and then hope the next month might be better. In theory this is better than nothing, as some business owners have no idea if they are profitable or not. However being able to have both the financial information and the broader company data on one page gives you insight into your progress. The ability to look at this month's data in relation to the average from the last period, and in view of the months prior, gives you a sense of control over your business. I always say *it is better to know you are doing badly,* as with knowledge comes the power to change and you can affect that change in real time. Much better this than merely hoping you are doing well. The following visual communicates the relationship between action and knowledge.

```
                    KNOWLEDGE
                        |
    1. The Fool         |    4. The Champion
                        |
                        |
 ───────────────────────────────────────────
    AVOID               |              ACT
                        |
    2. The Emu          |    3. The Negligent
                        |
                    IGNORANCE
```

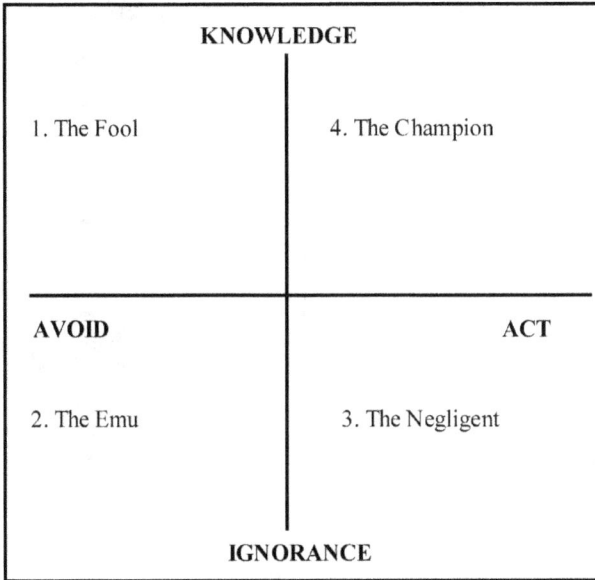

Figure 1.3: Knowledge in action

Quadrant 1. If we know what is happening but choose to avoid it, we are really just foolish.

Quadrant 2. If we choose to live in ignorance and avoid reality at all cost we are akin to the emu syndrome – head in the sand, tail in the air.

Quadrant 3. We have no knowledge of what is happening but we continue to act, thinking that action alone will save the day. We are negligent and can sink the entire ship.

Quadrant 4. We choose to know and then act accordingly – The Change Champion

WHAT DOES THE CUSTOMER WANT?

Let me give you a definition of customers that arise from chaotic workplaces – 'those we tolerate because they feed us.' How many times have you said, "Life would be so much easier if I didn't have to deal with people."

In any discussion around bringing order to business, it has to start with the client. What will make their life easier? What is it that they really want and need? If time is their most precious commodity, how much of it are we wasting through our internal inefficiencies? At the end of the day, and at the start for that matter, customers ARE our business. A happy customer will not only continue to use our services but will refer us to friends and family on an ongoing basis. An unhappy customer on the other hand will think twice about using us again and spread the word accordingly. With the advent of social media, that negativity can spread far and wide. You might have a $5000 client (where you provide an annual service for this amount) but a customer who sticks with you because of exceptional service and relationship potentially becomes a $50,000-$100,000 client over 10-20 years. Worth considering and building the customer into your process design... I would think (I know this is common sense but some, in their busy state, neglect to remember this). Also, when you consider the acquisition cost of a new customer, against a current client simply calling for new work or one of their friends contacting us from having been referred, the cost is virtually nothing.

Creating an efficient business, one in which the upstream effects of success flow in a continuous movement downstream through our business, must always have as its starting point the customer.

The best place to begin when considering this is to ask "what would I want?" If you were to use the services of your company, how would you like to be treated and what level of service and workmanship would you desire? Consider these:

1. Response times to my call or email

2. Friendliness and helpfulness on the phone

3. Time from booking an appointment, requesting a quote or booking the job to arrival

4. Knowing ahead of time what the costs, times, billings, etc. will be

5. Presentation of staff

6. Level of craftsmanship

7. Ease of doing business with

8. Is the company all about exceeding your expectations as a customer, just doing the job, or not really caring at all?

9. Would you like some added value that you hadn't been expecting?

10. If the results are substandard, how would you like to be responded to and what rectifying results would you want?

These are just some of the items to consider prior to looking at your company's internal processes, and to re-iterate, we can never underestimate the power of a customer's experience and corresponding satisfaction.

If we keep in mind what we would like to experience as the customer, it will assist us in creating an environment and a system that delivers excellence.

Having looked at what you would like to experience as the potential customer of your firm, let's now more accurately understand the particular needs and wants of your customers.

Gaining an understanding of your clients expectations is as simple as asking them. Consider these ideas:

1. **Surveys.** These can be sent out at the completion of the job to collect their feedback about your performance.

2. **Post work follow up.** One of the challenges in sending out surveys is getting people to respond to them. One of the ideas to counter this is to make a follow-up phone call the day after the job has been completed. One of the companies who service my car does this as well as anybody I know. After every service and as sure as the sun will rise, I receive a call from their client services department asking me if I was completely satisfied with the work they had performed the day before. Their workshop is incredibly busy but they have been able to personalize their process to ensure high customer satisfaction.

3. **Focus Groups.** These are conducted in a more organized meeting format, bringing together a select group of clients for the purpose of understanding how to better serve them.

I am surprised by how little thought goes into understanding what the customer wants. As I write this, I am staying at the wonderful Castle Inn in Newport, Rhode Island USA. They would have to be one of the most outstanding examples of designing process around the customer's needs and wants (and what the customer didn't know they needed and wanted). From daily temperature reports to the main news stories printed in A4 to preparing your bed prior to sleeping - all examples of a business going out of their way for the customer. And, all of us in service-based businesses can do similar. It just takes a little thought with a back end process to deliver. Will I be coming back to this hotel? You bet.

After gaining a thorough understanding of your customers expectations it is now time to turn toward creating our internal processes to meet these external customer requirements. The first step is to document your current business processes.

CASE STUDY - CUSTOMER COMPLAINTS

One business I consulted to was struggling with customer complaints. We identified the nature of the complaints and went about correcting the internal processes to meet the clients' expectations. We also tracked the complaints we received weekly. Interestingly, over a period of three months the complaints decreased. This company went on to post record earnings in the years to come, all from aligning internal process to customer expectations.

DOCUMENT CURRENT PROCESSES

Documenting process, though somewhat of an onerous task, can be hugely beneficial as you work through the following stages. Let's again start with the customer.

In this day and age, time is our most valuable commodity. Most of us dislike having to waste time on seemingly insignificant things. We like our meals brought out quickly (bring on the fast food and drive through convenience) and we disdain having to wait in any kind of queue. Have you ever stood in a midday line at the bank, only to discover that along with half the population on their lunch break the tellers decided to have theirs at the same time? Now there's a process to evaluate! We have grown to expect efficient service at all levels, choosing to go to the next shop or service provider if the one we are currently with is wasting our time. I want it and I want it now.

WHERE'S MY FOOD?

Sometime back I placed an order in a Melbourne restaurant and was shown to my table. Thirty minutes later the table next to me ordered their meals and had them on the table within fifteen minutes. (One of the orders was exactly the meal order I had placed). I motioned for the waiter and mentioned that I had placed my order 45 minutes ago. Apologetically he organised things very quickly. Upon paying my bill they reduced it by thirty percent and again were very apologetic. We all get it wrong at times but given the apologies and the discount I would definitely return.

Recently, I dealt with two separate companies within four weeks of each other. One was a telecommunications provider, the other an administration service. In both cases I emailed the person I was dealing with, requesting some information. In one case the response came back eight days later, the other three days later – both stating the reason that they had been off work and hadn't been able to access their email. As a customer, frankly I don't care about their reasons. What I wanted was a response and at least within twenty-four hours. In both cases, the businesses had failed to set up a system that provided a checking of individuals' emails by another worker. A business system must be created in order to serve the customers' expectations. If it doesn't, the customer will think twice about recommending you.

NOT THE BEST REFERRAL

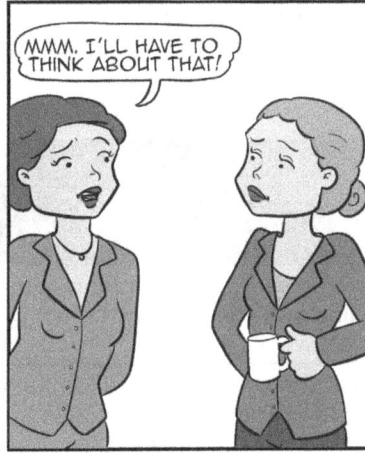

Customers choose to work with businesses that respect their time and if you can align your business processes around this fact, you will be on the leading edge of your industry. Think of same-day dry cleaning, rubbish removal from your home, express banking using the deposit box after hours, airline priority lanes. All these and a host of others have been created with a customer first approach.

So, with that in mind, let's have a look at the time a customer takes from their researching what company to get to do their work, right through the process to when they pay their bill. In the examples below I have used a plumbing company that can be interchanged for any service-based firm.

CUSTOMER PROCESS

PROCESS	Ave Time in Minutes	Ave time in days
Sarah researches plumbing companies online and calls a few of them getting prices	20	
Likes the sound of your company and talks to receptionist who says the plumber will call her back	10	
Waits for 2.5 days for the call back and decides to go ahead after talking to the plumber, in spite of the lead time being 10 days	10	3
Was told the plumber would be there at 1pm - it is now 2.15pm and they finally show (not having called to advise lateness). Meets with plumber to describe issue.	75	10

Half way through the job plumber disappears for an hour		
Plumber returns, no communication regarding having to go for an additional part and completes the job		
After the plumbers' departure, checks the original problem and all working well.	1	
Sees the mess on the floor that was left and has to clean it up	5	
Invoice arrives in the mail		17
Reads it and realizes she is being charged an extra hour for the time the tradesman wasn't onsite	5	
Puts call into company to be told that the plumber will have to phone her back	3	
Plumber returns call and advises her that it was for the spare part so is chargeable	7	2
Though not happy with it not being communicated on the day, decides to pay the bill at the end of the month. Wants to deduct cleaning time from their mess but chooses not to		17
Makes payment online	5	
Total time taken	141	49

Figure 1.4:Customer Process Matrixes

You can see through this customer process matrix that the company has effectively wasted Sarah's time due to their internal inefficiencies and lack of communication. Also, the service level is somewhat lacking (that's probably being too kind) and one would question if Sarah would think twice about calling this company the next time she had a plumbing issue. I know I wouldn't.

When consulting to service oriented businesses, this story is not uncommon. We, as business owners, must have a deep appreciation for the customers experience and do everything in our power to totally satisfy their expectations and more. The simple actions portrayed here of honoring their time, exceptional workmanship and communication go a long way toward customer happiness. And, a happy customer has many friends and associates in their personal sphere of influence to share both good and bad stories with. Make it the former for your customers. Let's now turn to documenting the current process within the business. We start again with listing every step from the customers' initial enquiry through to the payment of their bill.

INTERNAL PROCESS

Process	Who	Ave Time in Minutes	Ave time in days
Customer calls office to book job	Customer		
Take call and writes on loose paper	Receptionist	10	
Put paper into tray for plumbers	Receptionist		
Collect paper and calls client back to book job, writing into diary	Plumber	10	3
Travel to start job	Plumber	20	10
Job started	Plumber	N/A	
If parts required go to supplier and travel back	Plumber	20	
Job completed	Plumber	N/A	
Travel to next job	Plumber	N/A	
Job card completed within 7 days	Plumber	17	7
Job card given to receptionist to type up invoice	Plumber	5	1
Type invoice	Receptionist	5	2
Place invoice in tray for checking	Receptionist		
Invoice checked	Plumber	1	1
If error – discussion with receptionist	Plumber	2	
Invoice re-typed	Receptionist	5	1
Invoice put back into tray for checking	Receptionist		
Invoice re-checked	Plumber	2	2

Discussion with receptionist that invoice is good to be posted	Plumber	1	
Invoice printed and prepared for sending	Receptionist	2	1
Mail (inc. this invoice) taken to the post office	Receptionist	2	1
Total Time Taken		102	29

Figure 1.5: Internal Process Chart

You can see from the above chart that each job takes 102 minutes of internal process time from the initial customer call through to the time the invoice is processed and posted.

You will also notice that in terms of days, it is taking 29 days in total from the initial call for the job through to the time the invoice is posted. This doesn't include the time the customer takes to pay their invoice. For example, if you add an additional 21 days to this, you have a total of 50 days till the money is in your bank. I can hear some saying, "this would be a miracle to get to this level." Some companies can run between 90 to 120 days, which from a cash flow standpoint can be a disaster.

CASE STUDY - GETTING CASH TO FLOW

A trade service firm was struggling with cash flow, primarily due to blocked processes from the completion of the job to when the invoice was being sent. The initial average time was 90 days to get the invoice sent. Over a period of six months this was decreased to within seven days. We simply took this one area, process mapped it, found the waste and got to work on getting rid of the obstacles. We also aligned people to the key roles in the process to ensure that flow was happening throughout.

IDENTIFY YOUR MAJOR BLOCKAGES

Without doubt, a plumbing situation is probably the most apt analogy here. When we take the plug out of the sink, instead of the water disappearing quickly down the drain it sits still simply staring at us, not moving. A blocked drain. We call the plumber, they come and perform their magic and voilà, the water starts flowing again. Or we are on a freeway and it comes to a grinding halt. We travel for the next 15 minutes at a snail's pace and then finally, all clears and things are back to normal. These are analogous of business systems. All seems to be flowing perfectly then over a period of time we then notice that lead times on jobs are starting to increase, invoices that were being sent out daily are now at 14 days average and customer complaints and re-works seem to be increasing at a steady rate. Chaos descends as processes jam up.

Let's go back to the blocked drain scenario. Over time, one obstruction after another slowly builds in the unseen enclosure of the pipes. At first the water works its way around the refuse but slowly over time, as the rubbish builds, the water begins to slow until finally, no flow.

Business is no different.

Over time, slowly, in the hidden recesses of your business systems, obstructions enter the scene. It might be a new administration employee who lacks accuracy; ageing technology; decrease in administrative diligence; the low running tide of workplace enthusiasm and passion; a change in process that was never evaluated for its effectiveness. Slowly, these things all build upon the other resulting in obstructed and blocked systems. Just like the plumber, your job as business owner is first to identify these blockages and then secondly, to clear them.

A good way to identify where the potential obstructions are is to take a highlighting pen and work your way through the process that we reviewed earlier and, which for ease, I have reproduced below. Highlight the areas where things seem to back up or where you think things are taking too long and then ask the question, "How can we unblock this process point"?

See the following example

IDENTIFYING CURRENT BLOCKAGES

Process	Who	Ave Time in Minutes	Ave time in days
Customer calls office to book job	Customer		
Take call and writes on loose paper	Receptionist	10	
Put paper into tray for plumbers	Receptionist		
Collect paper and calls client back to book job, writing into diary	Plumber	10	3
Travel to start job	Plumber	20	10
Job started	Plumber	N/A	
If parts required go to supplier and travel back	Plumber	20	
Job completed	Plumber	N/A	
Travel to next job	Plumber	N/A	
Job card completed within 7 days	Plumber	17	7
Job card given to receptionist to type up invoice	Plumber	5	1
Type invoice	Receptionist	5	2
Place invoice in tray for checking	Receptionist		
Invoice checked	Plumber	1	1
If error – discussion with receptionist	Plumber	2	
Invoice re-typed	Receptionist	5	1
Invoice put back into tray for checking	Receptionist		
Invoice re-checked	Plumber	2	2

Discussion with receptionist that invoice is good to be posted	Plumber	1	
Invoice printed and prepared for sending	Receptionist	2	1
Mail (Inc. this invoice) taken to the post office	Receptionist	2	1
Total Time Taken		102	29

Figure 1.6: Identifying Current Blockages

There are a number of issues in the scenario above, but I have just highlighted the areas that are taking more than a day to complete that would be worth asking the harder questions about. Just as in the blocked drain scenario, until the obstruction is identified, we can't do anything about it. We can whine and complain, blaming others for the fault but until it's located, change cannot take place.

The challenge for most business owners is carving out the time to work through this process. It is onerous, challenging, and slow at times. This is where using an employee, manager or external consultant with high detail orientation or someone that can spot inefficiencies quickly can be useful for the process.

CASE STUDY – HAPPY WIFE, HAPPY LIFE

After conducting a review of the current systems and processes for a builder doing high-end renovations, we discovered a major obstruction in his getting invoices out in a timely manner and which had a direct impact on his cash flow. He would write the invoices out by hand and give them to his significant other who was already working a forty-hour week for another firm. She struggled to get them out quickly and certainly wasn't a boon to their relationship. We decided to re-route the process by purchasing an electronic pen from simPRO. With this in place, when my client had handwritten the invoice with the new pen, he ticked the 'send' section on the pre- ordered invoice form and a copy of the invoice was sent as a PDF file – via email – to his bookkeeper, thus bypassing the 'blockage' and converting it to text. A simple but effective clearing strategy. And...better than a bunch of flowers at that point!!

2

Process Redesign

CREATING FLOW

Before we dive into redesigning the process let's talk briefly about setting improvement goals in relation to the earlier Key Performance Indicator (KPI) chart we spoke of in chapter one, as this will provide a foundational key as we progress.

IMPROVEMENT GOALS

Just as each road trip has a start and a finish with mid-way stopping points (milestones of the journey), business is really no different. When discussing the implementation of change within our business, understanding the starting point (the baseline) with key achievement goals and milestones along the way are essential for momentum and monitoring progression. To this point, we've talked about the use of the KPI chart and the need to identify current processes. These give us a starting place – the understanding of our current business performance in terms of numbers and process, customer satisfaction levels, etc.

With regards to the setting of improvement goals, my personal approach is to set something that you feel is achievable within a certain time frame. It might be a 12% increase in revenues over the next 12 months, decreasing job reworks by 30% or converting 5% more quotes into sales in the next quarter.

The great thing about using a KPI chart shown in Chapter 1 is that you can capture:

- Where you are now
- Where you would like to be
- Monitor your progress monthly against the starting place and the destination (improvement goal)
- Make just-in-time changes based on the data

The main advantage of doing it this way is you get to make changes in 'almost' real time. Entering your key results at the end of each month enables you to:

1. Ascertain whether the change you are implementing is improving your condition or weakening it

2. Make changes then and there rather than waiting for your annual visit with your accountant (and get advice in retrospect) – valuable as it is

3. Shift the goal posts if you fly past the original ones you set

4. See the month past in relation to the whole year not just in isolation. Many business owners and managers get their financial reports at month-end, review them and then plough on. They are never reviewed in context of the broader picture and the accountants' annual review is often too late. The damage is done

5. Share the broader information with your team, empowering them to make changes as they need to happen

6. Establish goals and track results in various business departments

Capturing your current business performance through the:

-   Setting of improvement goals
-   Monitoring your progress monthly
-   Making just in time changes where required

will assist in keeping your business on track and prevent unseen slippage.

REDESIGN BASED ON IMPROVEMENT GOALS

Now we have set our improvement goals let's review the current processes table and work through each blockage in order. I have copied it here for sake of ease in working this through.

IDENTIFYING CURRENT BLOCKAGES

Process	Who	Ave Time in Minutes	Ave time in days
Customer calls office to book job	Customer		
Take call and writes on loose paper	Receptionist	10	
Put paper into tray for plumbers	Receptionist		
Collect paper and calls client back to book job, writing into diary	Plumber	10	3
Travel to start job	Plumber	20	10
Job started	Plumber	N/A	
If parts required go to supplier and travel back	Plumber	20	
Job completed	Plumber	N/A	
Travel to next job	Plumber	N/A	
Job card completed within 7 days	Plumber	17	7
Job card given to receptionist to type up invoice	Plumber	5	1
Type invoice	Receptionist	5	2
Place invoice in tray for checking	Receptionist		
Invoice checked	Plumber	1	1
If error - discussion with receptionist	Plumber	2	
Invoice re-typed	Receptionist	5	1
Invoice put back into tray for checking	Receptionist		
Invoice re-checked	Plumber	2	2

Discussion with receptionist that invoice is good to be posted	Plumber	1	
Invoice printed and prepared for sending	Receptionist	2	1
Mail (inc. this invoice) taken to the post office	Receptionist	2	1
Total Time Taken		102	29

BLOCKAGE ONE – SCHEDULING

Initial call from customer and the writing down the message for the plumber to return phone call.

Redesign thoughts

a. One idea would be to implement or use the current software you have in place or purchasing software that is tailor made to your industry. Most who have this software in place don't utilize it to its fullest. Reviewing our process blockage list (and whether we already have the software or whether we might need to purchase a system), we make the decision to have the receptionist trained in order to enter the customer data and job details directly into the software. In turn, this enables the tradesman to view all incoming calls and pending jobs for scheduling on his laptop or iPad wherever he is during the day. If there was a set time every day for the tradesperson to view the incoming calls and pending job, she could then commit to calling everyone back within 24 hours thus reducing the call back time from 3 days to 1 day.

Better still, if the receptionist was also given the authority to book jobs directly into the schedule, (or a dedicated scheduler was employed for this sole purpose) this alleviates the need for the tradesperson to make the callback thus reducing the 3-day call return to same day. This is where process redesign meets customers' expectations perfectly. They call, you book, job done. No waiting, no games of phone tag, no being left in time and space.

Another scenario here if there is no electronic system in place, it could be that the receptionist writes all incoming calls into one book. The tradesperson makes the commitment that every after-noon between 5- 6pm he will return all calls and book all incoming work requests. Simple, I know, but effective when discipline prevails. Further to this scenario, if the receptionist has a whiteboard where all scheduled jobs are displayed near them, they simply book the job in on the spot, writing it onto the board.

The more steps you can delete in the process, going from incom-ing call to job booking, whenever possible on the spot, creates great customer service and prevents you from the issues that are created from the loose paper and call back scenarios.

Blockage Two – Job card completion

This is one of the major blockages of cash flow and obviously, the sooner you can get the completed job card converted to an invoice and sent to the customer, the sooner the money arrives in your bank.

Redesign thoughts

A simple solution here is for the tradesperson to complete the job card at the end of each job. The benefits being:

1. **Completed on-site and then reducing the current 7 day process to 12 hours.** One idea here is the implementation of electronic processing of the job card from site to office. I have seen three methods used here.

   a. The use of electronic pen and dedicated job card forms. This is a very effective method of getting the job card back to base immediately after the jobs completion. The tradesperson completes the job card just like they would using the standard pen and paper but in this form, there is a send box on the bottom of the form and as soon as that has been touched, the job card turns up back at the office in electronic format. The interesting thing about this method is that the pen has standard ink in it and writes on actual paper. The pen has a camera in it and the forms are specifically designed to be used with the actual pen. When used with the appropriate scheduling software, the job card, which was completed in handwriting then converts to a typed format in the software, thus reducing the need to have to re-type the whole card.

   b. Using laptops or iPads essentially achieve the same as the above, but are more effective due to the tradesperson typing directly into the software.

c. One company I know of have their tradesman take a photo of the handwritten job card and email it back from their Smartphone. Not as effective as the above methods, but certainly gets the cards back same day.

2. **Reduction of errors.** On the above chart we noted that there was an apparent error rate with the receptionist converting the job card to the invoice. Completing these same day and then reviewing with the receptionist can reduce this due to it being done while still fresh in the tradespersons mind.

3. **Additional billable time.** When completing a job card on site the tradesperson spends an average of ten minutes on its completion. If, for example, your company is completing thirty jobs per week, this equates to an additional 300 minutes per week (or 5 hours). Over the course of a year this gives you an additional 260 hours of billable time. If your hourly rate is $80 this creates an additional $20,800 in extra revenue. This should be enough motivation to complete the job card at the end of each job. It also increases the value of the tradesperson, as more of their time is billable.

CASE STUDY – THE TRIAL OF AN IPAD

A plumber, having existing scheduling software in place, decided to trial this with one of their tradesman but took it one step further. The owner purchased an iPad and taught the tradesman how to use it for job card completion. He was amazed. What often took days for the job cards to be completed now happened at the end of the job and was back in the office within 60 seconds of completion due to the electronic transmission. His turnaround for invoicing was down to five minutes of the jobs completion (and had added an extra ten minutes of billable time to every invoice).

BLOCKAGE THREE – INVOICING

We have a couple of issues in the current process. One is that there is a nine-day delay in getting invoices out to the customer from the time the job card has been completed assuming in this case that there are errors. Let's work through this.

If we established standard times for invoicing completion and sending, we could reduce this down to three days. This is a case of raising the bar of our company standards in the invoicing department and also in the diligence of the tradesperson in checking the awaiting invoices at day's end. By setting tighter time frames and increased expectations of our staff, it creates a culture of discipline and focus, much of which is lacking in many organizations. It also puts money into our bank at a faster rate.

The other issue in the blockage above is the invoicing error rate.

I worked with a company where errors were costing an approximate $20,000 per annum; another where 16% of invoices going out had errors on them. Two of the main reasons for us taking the measurements on the second situation above was the amount of calls received by customers saying their invoice was wrong, and the other being that the general manager of the firm was taking 5-6 hours per week to check the invoices prior to being sent to the customer. This amounts to one word – WASTE!

What we also found was that the errors caused by administration were due to them going too fast in the processing of them and not taking time to double check the accuracy. By the simple implementation of the processing personnel slowing down to review the invoice against the job card, checking for their own errors reduced the error rate by half in the first three months with further progress made as they progressed.

To complete this area of creating flow, let's look at a redesigned process from our work thus far.

NEW PROCESS TABLE

Process	Who	Ave Time in Minutes	Ave time in days
Customer calls office to book job	Customer		
Take calls and books directly into job schedule	Receptionist	15	
Call customer to confirm job on the day	Plumber	2	
Travel to start job	Plumber	20	10
Job started	Plumber	N/A	
If parts required go to supplier and travel back	Plumber	20	
Job completed	Plumber	N/A	1
Travel to next job	Plumber	N/A	
Job card completed same day	Plumber	17	1
Job card converted to invoice and posted to customer	Plumber	5	1
Total Time Taken		79	13

Figure 1.7: New Process Table

You can see that we have reduced the process steps considerably with reductions of minutes from 102 to 79 per job process and then 29 days to 13 days from the customers initial call to getting the invoice sent. Obviously, in the above example, there is more work to do in terms of lead times and the waste experienced by having to go to suppliers but we have made a good start.

I think an important thing to note here is that often when we start the process there seems so many areas that need improvement and it can be quite overwhelming. The key is to always identify the one or two main areas that, if corrected, will bring significant changes and impact other more marginal areas.

As a final note, many businesses struggle with the management of cash flow. If you look at this as a symptom of process disorder, and we go back and fix the blocked processes, it then allows cash to flow in more easily.

> **The key is to always identify the one or two main areas that if corrected, will bring significant changes and impact other more marginal areas...**

3

Policies, Processes, Procedures and Systems

THE DIFFERENCE BETWEEN CHAOS AND ORDER

What you started with in business five years ago or even six months ago won't necessarily be applicable for today. Business requires constant monitoring and ongoing improvement to keep up with the ever-increasing demands and the constant changes in the business environment. The statement that Marshall Goldsmith is well known for "What got you here, won't get you there" could be no truer. The responsibilities of leadership in both creating chaos (increased sales and front-end activity) with the corresponding order that is required in back end systems and processes increase as the business progresses. A one-person company whose sole existence is to provide a job and income for the owner is substantially different to a firm that is growing in sales and personnel. Figure 1.8 demonstrates the relationship between demand and improvement initiative. If little demand then little needs to be done in the way of improvement if things are working well. Things can always be improved, but the necessity for it is, obviously, lower. As demand increases, the change needs to be commensurate with the ongoing requirements.

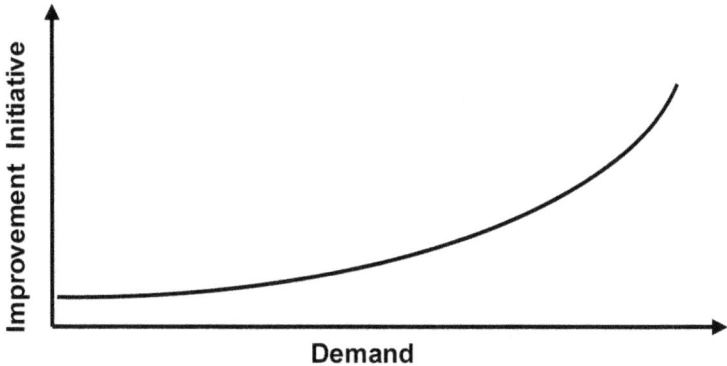

Fig 1.8: Demand Initiative Curve

One of foundational aspects for largely enhancing the streamlining effect brought to business – effectively smashing the bottleneck – is in having each area documented in terms of Policies, Procedures, Processes, and Systems. And if you are running a solo operation or with one or two others, the need is a lot lower than if you are a thousand-person firm. As I said, the demand and improvement requirements are interrelated.

Being able to keep alert by utilising key data for monitoring and then acting to make changes in real time is management excellence. Too many though, in attempting to keep up with the chaos of a growing business, simply give in. Cash flow is good, things aren't broke so they don't bother fixing anything. My observation, and in particular of those companies that are growing at a reasonable rate, is that those who get caught up in front-end demand, having to keep up with managing the chaos and who ,subsequently, neglect the active implementation of improvement initiative pay for it in the end. Those payments might include employee loss, stress related health issues, profit drops, customer complaints, cash flow challenges and the like. This final chapter deals with the various distinctions required in the administrative back end of companies and organisations. Having well thought through and documented systems, processes etc., along with the discipline of the constant upgrading of these to meet current demand is part of the order and resulting success equation. The establishment and document-ing of such is necessary, both to keep everyone on the same page and also where one person leaves and a new recruit steps in. This way they can follow the standards set down by the company thus minimizing error.

DISTINCTIONS

Policy: The guiding principles and rules used to ensure the obser-vance and consistent application of a company's strategic plan. These would include management expectations, philosophies, company mission and vision statements, laws and regulations and industry standards, etc.

Process: The systematic series of activities required to produce a desired outcome, typically converting inputs into outputs. Process maps are often used as a way of tracking the flow of actions involved from one point to another. They convey who is responsible at the various stages and reflect trigger points for when the next step comes into play.

Procedure: The course of actions required to effectively implement part of a process. It should include instructions and a concise description of duties and responsibilities for target users. Procedures portray a clear series of steps for the completion of tasks.

System: The integration or path of policies, procedures and processes implemented to achieve the smooth and efficient operation of a business.

On the following pages you will see examples of each of these.

POLICY DOCUMENT

Policy Title: Customer Service Policy		Print Date: 1st October 2012
Document #: POLCLI001	Prepared By: Jane Smith	Date Prepared: 1st September 2012
Revision #: N/A	Reviewed By: Ray Hodge	Date Reviewed: 15th Sept 2012
Effective Date: 1st November 2012	Approved By: ABC Managing Director	Date Approved: 20th Sept 2012
Standard/s if applicable:		

Policy Statement: It is ABC Pty Ltd policy to ensure new customers receives the best, most efficient and effective service at all times from all members of ABC Company staff. We are committed to giving our customers only the best in service and products and to exceed their expectations whenever we can. We are committed to develop and maintain exceptional customer relations built on mutual trust, respect and loyalty. We expect all employees to correctly identify our customers' expectations, responding to changing trends and demands, and are devoted to pursuing quality as a way of life at ABC Pty Ltd.

Objective: The objective of this policy is to ensure all new and existing customers receive the best quality service from ABC staff at all times

Scope: The scope of this policy relates to new and existing customers and all staff of ABC company

Name:	Responsibility/Role:
John Doe	Implementation of policy by customer service staff
ABC Managing Director	Implementation of policy by all supervisors and managers

Related Records and Forms: The related records and forms for this policy are New Client File opening Procedure CLI001/another002/another003 and are stored/filed at the Customer Service Dept. at Head Office.

Revision:	Date:	Description of changes:	Requested by:

Copies distributed to: Customer Service Dept., Human Resources Dept., Central Admin Services

Fig 1.9: Policy Document

PROCESS EXAMPLE

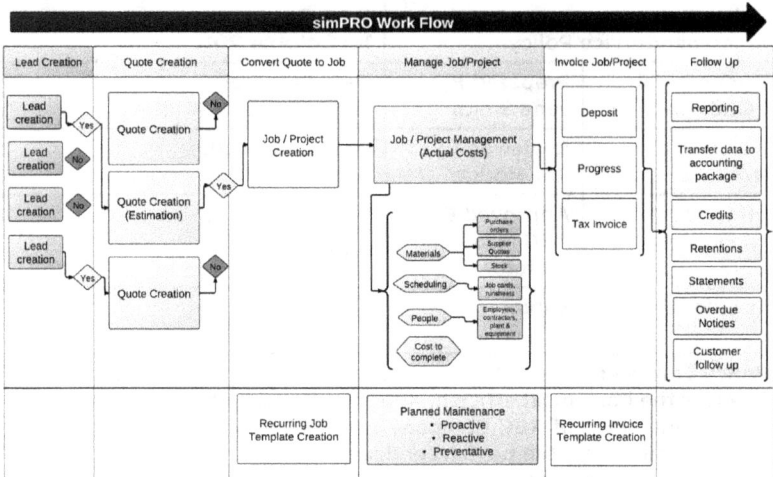

Fig 1.10: Process Example

PROCEDURE EXAMPLE

New Client File
Purpose: The purpose of this procedure is to provide guidelines for ensuring all new clients are allocated a file containing accurate, up-to-date records and information on their requirements, products, services and any issues or complaints. This file is to be used by ABC staff to ensure they have up to date and accurate information to ensure the new client receives the best possible service at all times.
Scope: The scope of this procedure relates to management, administrative and customer service staff and excludes only those staff who do not have access to company or customer files.
Related Policies: The policy of ABC Company in relation to this procedure is 'to ensure our customers receive the best, most efficient and effective service at all times from all members of ABC Company staff.'
Related Records and Documents: The related records and forms for this procedure is the New Customer Record Request and is stored/filed at the Customer Service Department – Customer files and in the Customer database.
Responsible Persons: Responsible for implementation and follow through of this procedure are Dan Robinson -Customer Records Administrative Assistant; Jane Doe- Customer Service Supervisor and John Aber- Customer Relations Director.
Procedure: 1. Ensure all contact information for the new client is accurate by testing phone numbers, - emails and checking the address. 2. Open Customer Database. 3. Open 'New Customer Record' – click relevant button in database. 4. A new customer number will be allocated by the database. 5. Input relevant contact details in appropriate named fields of 'Customer Contact Details' form. 6. Input customer communication details and dates in 'Customer Communication' form. 7. Input customer orders and products in 'Customer Orders' page. 8. Once completed, request your supervisor check all entries and approve new customer record. 9. Email Customer Relations Director with notification of New Customer Record number, orders and report

Title/Subject	Approved by	Date	Version	Page No.

Fig 1.11: Procedure Example

SYSTEM EXAMPLE

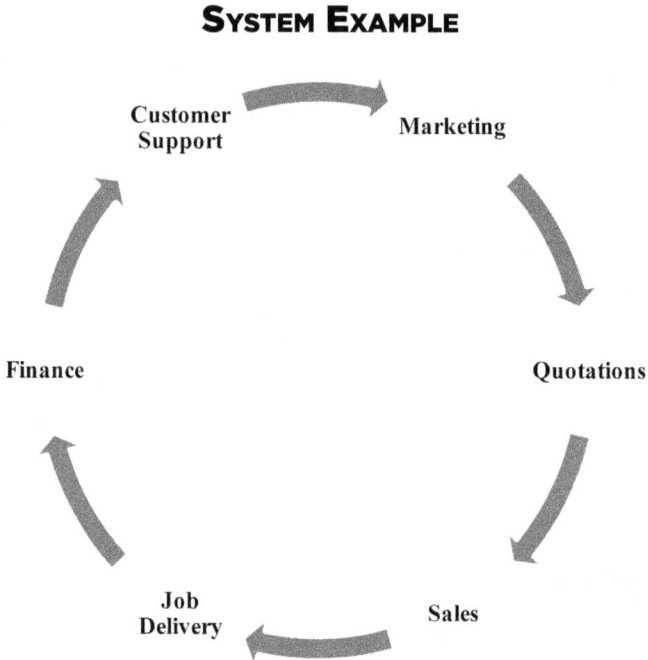

Fig 1.12: System Example

As I said earlier, by documenting and implementing the above, businesses also greatly reduce the risks of disruption caused from staff turnover or losing key personnel for any reason. Spreading the knowledge base and using properly written business systems, ensures any member of staff or management can step in and take over at any time by reading 'instructions' for any particular job. It is also good to train as many staff and management in as many different jobs as possible should the occasion arise when they are required to step in. Job swap is a good way for staff and management to experience other duties and responsibilities whilst testing your documented processes to check how easy they are to follow.

WRITING EXCELLENT BUSINESS SYSTEMS

Even if you already provide your staff with documented policies, procedures and process instructions, one of the questions I'd ask is: "were they involved in writing them and do you expect them to let you know when a process breaks down or isn't performing at it potential best?"

Most staff or line managers will endeavour to sort issues out themselves without bothering the owner or senior management, especially if the process or procedure is one you have written and are expecting them to follow. You are more likely to find out when the issue has *seriously* affected productivity, profitability, customer service, quality and staff morale and, most times, this is too late.

The best way to ensure buy in, from every level of the organization, is to first listen. Listen to those on the floor working the process; hear their views, ideas and concerns. Make them part of the business systems creation. Collaborate with your staff in designing and writing good business systems and you'll find increased engagement at every level.

Team meetings are an excellent way of ensuring all those involved in a process are actually part of its initial design and ongoing success. This not only promotes effectiveness but also builds commitment, loyalty, and a sense of achievement in your team. Create a team responsible for ongoing reviews. Have regular team meetings to evaluate the effectiveness and efficiency of your processes and procedures. Ensure you give these meetings your full commitment, a high priority item included in your schedule.

Choose whichever method of documenting and indexing your policies and processes that works best for your particular company. Flowcharts work well although many companies prefer to use simple numbered instructions.

Keep processes, procedures, and systems as working (live) documents, easy to update, modify and distribute. Ensure they are easily accessible by all staff and are easy to understand. There is no point creating complicated procedures and processes using language that your staff can't relate to. Keep system documents simple, effective, readable and usable and, keep listening to your staff as to how best to increase effectiveness.

FROM THE SHELF TO THE SHOP FLOOR

It is one thing to have nice looking procedure manuals lining your bookshelf accompanied by beautifully framed policy statements on your reception wall but... how do we get them implemented from the shelf to the floor? Here are a few ideas.

- Ensure that the person responsible for the particular process has the relevant procedures on hand

- Develop a company intranet that makes them readily available in electronic format to all employees

- Create videos, again available on the intranet, for visual explanation on how to fulfil a particular procedure

- Upon initial implementation and for ongoing reviews that procedures are being followed, having team members use the procedure document as a checklist to indicate they have fulfilled each step can give you a good indication that things are flowing as they should. Honesty by the team member is the key in this process. Also having an area on the document for the person to note what isn't working or could be done better can be a good idea for further tweaks to the process.

- Ensure management are responsible for the oversight and execution of these with responsibilities and corresponding performance measures documented in their position descriptions

- Employ or assign a 'process champion'. See following case study.

- Measurements. Relate the performance of particular processes and procedures to your Key Performance Indicators. An example might be that one indicator is the time taken from a quote request to a proposal/quotation being sent to the customer. If you know that by following the stages of the process involved with the corresponding procedures for each stage, the time frame will be 3 days. If it blows out beyond this, the KPI chart will alert you to this, enabling management to quickly rectify the issue and also to find where the flow is breaking down.

CASE STUDY – THE PROCESS CHAMPION

A professional firm's significant bottom line shift, in a very short period of time, came primarily from focusing on its process efficiencies. One of the smart things they implemented was the appointment of a 'process champion'. Someone that was already on staff and that exhibited high attention to detail. One of her responsibilities was to ensure the processes and procedures in place were actually implemented (from shelf to floor). They worked with the relevant team members in ensuring process was being followed, making the necessary tweaks and changes when the flow of process became obstructed. They then recorded the corresponding results onto the KPI chart for weekly evaluation with management.

Their work typically followed this pattern:

1. Evaluate and measure

2. Establish improvement goal

3. Make necessary changes to current processes, flow etc.

4. Record and evaluate outcomes

5. Start at number 1 again

In Conclusion

The systemizing of a business in no small feat, especially when things are in chaos. Hoever, I have seen firsthand, time and time again, when businesses prioritise the activity of bringing order and smashing the bottlenecks – whether taking the task on themselves or assigning it to the likes of a 'process champion' – flow begins to happen. Often it is over a period of weeks the effects of a process redesign are realized. Errors start to disappear, staff becomes happier, cash begins to flow, quotes are issued in shorter time frames, lead times are reduced and so forth.

I liken the growth of a business to an expanding family. When it is just two people in the honeymoon period of their relationship, things are easy. Life flows. Add the complexities of joint home ownership, children (and all the responsibilities that come with it), and life becomes subsequently different. Just as a growing family with all its demands are ever adapting and bringing order to periodic chaos, a growing business is not too dissimilar.

The result of our success is often reflected by the increase in both new business and repeat business. Being able to constantly adapt and stay at the forefront of things, bring order to the chaos, identifying bottlenecks and dealing with them quickly is paramount to the ongoing 'flow' of the business. I wish you every success.

Appendix

Case Study

By Ray Hodge

Introduction

This case study incorporates the ideas put forth in this book and is representative of the significant effects on a business when process redesign and the subsequent application of such is implemented. Upon completion of the project simPRO software requested a study be completed, thus the software references.

Stimson Plumbing and Ray Hodge have worked together for the past fifteen months to reduce the bottlenecks it was experiencing in its business. Stimson was struggling with overload, and the systems and procedures it had in place weren't keeping up with the growth it had been experiencing. Ray was requested to assist in streamlining Stimson's workflow as it related to its operations and integrate the existing simPRO software it was using into the process improvement.

STAGE ONE: ANALYSIS – CURRENT PROCESS AND RESULTS

In the early stages, we spent time ascertaining what the key challenges were and establishing the current results they were experiencing in the various areas they were struggling with. The simPRO reporting was a key part of gaining the relevant data to measure the current results. It also helped us understand where the key blockages were. Once we had this information, a Key Performance Indicator chart was established with the prior year's performance included. Areas that were listed included:

- Financial information
- Plumbers' personal productivity in percentage terms, which demonstrated the amount of chargeable time against the actual time, worked.
- Job cards waiting to be invoiced
- Error rates/complaints
- Job numbers
- Average dollar sale
- Quotes submitted to those won
- Sales levels in the various categories they were working in

Once this information had been entered, an average was taken of the previous period with improvement goals established. A key part of this stage was to use a business mapping process to understand the current workflow in the organisation. Every process from the initial customer contact to the customers resulting satisfaction (or lack

thereof) was documented with corresponding time frames attrib-
uted. It was found that an estimated 143 minutes were being taken
to internally process a job from start to finish. Current job roles and
the corresponding key tasks were also documented.

STAGE TWO: PROCESS REDESIGN

The second stage of our work was to redesign the company's internal
process in alignment to the customers' expectations and experience.
simPRO was again, an integral part of this redesign and a detailed
business process map was used in the redesign phase. We sought to
eliminate all double handling and any wasted effort and time in the
process. Some of the redesign areas included:

- Five major process stages reduced to four
- The redefining of employee roles
- Taking out all-unnecessary steps in the process and combin-
  ing steps where possible. An example of this was having
  reception logging the job directly into simPRO rather than
  writing on a piece of paper and placing in a tray for someone
  else to collect thus creating time delays and lack of control
  over jobs
- One person to schedule all jobs (rather than different people
  being involved)

The time taken to complete stages one and two was approximately
six weeks. Having all the available data in simPRO amounted to a
huge time saving in this phase.

STAGE THREE: IMPLEMENTATION

Once the business process mapping redesign had been completed, we then identified the key areas that needed to be acted upon first. The team at simPRO were involved in regular communication during this phase, assisting us in getting the process and data required for the implementation of the new processes to gain the maximum results we were after. The first six months were reasonably challenging for the whole firm as the changes took place. Some of the key changes included:

- The purchase and integration of the electronic simPRO pens for all plumbers

- Re-allocation of roles were implemented with a dedicated job scheduling position introduced (this was one of the major implementation challenges)

- Additional training was completed with simPRO to assist in the reorganisation.

STAGE FOUR: MONITORING AND RECORDING PROGRESS

As things progressed through the implementation phase, recording the changes and monitoring the new process was essential. The initial Key Performance Chart from phase one was utilised to provide ongoing recording of results in the major change areas. Keeping up to date, relevant data (again sourced from simPRO) assisted in the understanding of what changes were working and what required further development. Customer surveys were also reviewed to ascertain the impact that the internal company changes were having on the customers' satisfaction levels.

STAGE FIVE: MANAGE NEW PROCESSES

As the implementation and monitoring phases progressed, we continued to manage this by incremental improvements to the changes we had made. Other areas of management and analysis in this phase were:

- Analysis of sales in the various revenue categories
- Job profitability
- Quote-to-sale ratios and tweaking the quotation process

RESULTS

The major results to date are as follows:

- An estimated saving of 83 minutes per job which equated to 51 hours per week of additional time available by current employees
- Major process bottlenecks removed
- All staff know EXACTLY what their responsibilities are with procedures and flow charts to follow
- Profitability increased 134% over the previous financial year
- 9% reduction in labour expenses
- 6% reduction in cost of sales
- 29% deccrease in job cards waiting to be invoiced

- Defined job roles in conjunction with the redesigned process map in conjunction with the simPRO system
- 17% decrease in aged receivables
- 55% decrease in cost of defects
- 7% increase in average dollar sale

It is also worthwhile to note that Stimson Plumbing won the Gold Category for business process for their Regional Business Excellence Awards, and in the recent awards won Gold for the Information process category (which relates to the KPI work accomplished) and Silver in Business Process Management. Out of all submissions, they won the Silver award overall.

In the words of Jody Monaghan, Stimson's General Manager, *'the combination of our desire for excellence and quality delivery of service to our clients, having simPRO as our central software system in conjunction with Ray's consulting work has taken our business to another level'.*

WHAT OTHERS ARE SAYING ABOUT RAY'S WORK

"Ray Hodge spoke at many of our events in last years industry briefing nights. I could tell he knew what he was talking about and was able to keep the members fully engaged in his presentation. His speaking led us to request that he work with the association to consult to our sales and marketing department. Apart from the significant improvement from his work with us he also identified key future areas to help us in our ongoing quest for to be the industry leaders."

- **OLIVER JUDD - EXECUTIVE DIRECTOR: NECA NSW**

"When Ray initially began working with us we had significant challenges and bottlenecks in the areas of paperwork and cashflow. I felt like I was behind all the time. Over a period of a few months, systems were created and implemented, our tradesmen adopted the new way of doing things, invoicing was happening quicker and the chaos started to ease. What is significant that we couldn't see at the time is that the results in cashflow turnaround enabled us to fund a million dollar job that we could never have done previously out of business funds."

- **KELLY MULLINS - J MULLINS PLUMBING**

"We employed the services of Ray Hodge to increase the effectiveness of our management team and also to assist in our ambitious goal of doubling our business within the next three years. Ray's work and the associated outcomes have been significant resulting in taking our current management team (who were already good at what they did) to the next level of maturity in their roles and personal confidence. This also involved the clarification and alignment of their future roles in relation to our expansion plans and repositioning accordingly; dealing with the 'dead wood' in the place; increased clarity on the strategic direction of the company which has resulted in two new acquisitions and one joint venture, improving revenues by a projected 12% in the short to midterm; approximately 50% shift in our account managers sales performance. It is also worth noting that I have increased time to work on the future of the business given that I now have a team who continue to carry on with the day to day business affairs."

- DEAN NELSON - MANAGING DIRECTOR. HOISTING EQUIPMENT SPECIALISTS (VIC) PTY LTD

"In the last few months of working with Ray we have seen significant results within our business in terms of streamlining our processes and workflow along with the effectiveness of having redefined the supervisory roles. This also involved ensuring that our current job management system was being fully utilised that we are still in process with. Once the initial stage was completed we then added a marketing focus to our improvement endeavours. From this we have seen our an estimated 65% increase in work over the last 4 months with one client returning to us representing approximately 50% of our current revenues. Given the increase of work we are now having to plan the next stage of growth."

- BRENDAN FINDLAY - FINDLAY ENGINEERING PTY LTD

"Rays individual consulting work has assisted in keeping me focused, setting up systems and reviewing budgets to keep my firm's 'producers' accountable. Ray has also assisted greatly in providing advice and support during a transition period where the previous business owner left under unfavourable circumstances. The result for this last financial year is an approximate 25% increase in turnover when compared to the previous 2 financial years. Prior to working with Ray, the business had seen no growth or increase in staff performance."

- PETER McCARTNEY - SPRANKLIN McCARTNEY LAWYERS

"We have worked with Ray Hodge these past eight months. Our business had grown to a point where we really needed assistance with the systems and related people who interacted with the various procedures. Ray's help has been invaluable in that we have achieved a more fully process driven business with significant reductions in turnaround time frames, particularly relating to administration, with quoting times reduced by half. Increased role and responsibility clarification of staff and management along with the introduction of a new job management system Ray introduced us to has also helped this to become reality. His ability to spot the key issues has been immensely helpful and are grateful for his assistance."

- BRETT MATTHEWS - RNM SOLUTIONS PTY LTD

"Working with Ray has been beneficial in helping us to effectively look at our business costs and analyse them so that we were able to break it down and really discard our inefficiencies. This has given us the confidence in our own budgeting and structure, that if we wish to expand further, we will do this with confidence; that our costs will be kept to a minimum and we will be using the most cost effective ways to expand but still minimise our overheads."

- ANNETTE EDWARDS - RED SOIL CONSTRUCTIONS

"Ray Hodge was engaged to help the directors of Roberts & Cowling analyse their business with an objective party. This enabled us to identify bottle necks and design new efficient systems to overcome these bottlenecks. Ray then assisted us to establish and put in place these systems. All staff have become engaged and business seems so much easier. The business now is growing rapidly..."

**- BEN ROBERTS M ACCT BBUS (MAN)
PARTNER ROBERTS & COWLING**